TENANTS

OR,

WHEN THE HORNET ARRIVES

Nat Cassidy

BROADWAY PLAY PUBLISHING INC
224 E 62nd St, NY, NY 10065
www.broadwayplaypub.com
info@broadwayplaypub.com

First edition: October 2017
I S B N: 978-0-88145-740-7

Book design: Marie Donovan
Page make-up: Adobe InDesign
Typeface: Palatino

CHARACTERS & SETTING

JEFF, *male, 30s-40s, innocent, well-meaning, thinks himself an ally*

M, *male or female or nonbinary, 20s-40s, a survivor*

G, *male or female or ninbinary, 20s-40s, a caretaker*

Note: M *and* G *can be played by any gender, provided they are* not *a heterosexual couple.*

Setting: An apartment in New York City. It could easily be yours.

A NOTE ON THE, UM, SPECIAL EFFECTS

So, as you'll see, there's an effect halfway through this play that requires some ingenuity. Inspired designers might have a much better way to tackle it, but here's an idea to at least get you started: prepare a costume for the actor playing M with lots of red-colored Velcro all along its back and shoulders. Also cover the top of the cot with Velcro. Seam the cot and the costume with clumps of gunk, so that when the actor lays on the cot, it looks like s/he is glued in place. Ideally, this will keep the actor convincingly in place, but also allow for a quick change and for a safe escape in case of emergencies. It should also give you a GREAT ripping sound when they finally tear themselves free. Of course, the reason you want the Velcro to be red is it'll also look like torn flesh. What a nice play you've decided to produce.

A NOTE ON PRONOUNS

It was absolutely my intent that the characters of G and M not be bound by any sort of gender type in writing, as long as they are not a heterosexual couple. Any definitive gender pronouns used herein are either the result of my own accidental editorial oversight, or are done so purely for convenience of reading/comprehending the script, so please feel free to change them to whatever's appropriate to your specific production.

Moreover, the Lord your God will send the hornet among them until even the survivors who hide from you have perished.
Deuteronomy 7:20

Foxes have holes, and birds of the air have nests, but the Son of Man has nowhere to lay his head.
Matthew 8:20

For Kelley, on our newest adventure.

Scene One

(*An apartment living room. Nothing special, could be anyone's apartment. It's not super huge, it's not super new. It's just a home.*)

(*JEFF FERRELL is moving out, packing up everything. He, too, is nothing special.*)

(*He surveys his stuff. He seems a little sad. Distracted. What's going on in his head?*)

(*Most of his stuff is in boxes now. Boxes are piled high. There's still a couch and coffee table. There's also a floor lamp that looks memorable somehow. The kitchen is offstage, but we can see the entrance.*)

(*The front door is onstage. There is a knock. He goes to it.*)

(*M and G are on the other side. They are a same sex couple.*)

M: Hi! //Sorry to

G: Hi!
Is it okay if we

JEFF: Uh

G: We're

M: We're here to look at the apartment

JEFF: Oh. Hi.

M: Hi!
Rogelio (*"Ro-hey-lio"*) said it'd be okay if we stopped by

G: Is this bad timing

JEFF: No, no, come on in.

G: You sure? Rogelio said it'd be okay if

JEFF: Yeah, come on in.

G: Thank you!
Oh, nice—look at this living room!

(G *and* M *enter and start to look around. After a brief moment,* M *realizes the rudeness.*)

M: Oh, God, I'm sorry. I'm M, this is G.

JEFF: M and G. Hi.

G: Hi.

JEFF: Sorry about the clutter

G: Oh, God, you should see our place!
We can totally come back if this is a bad time

JEFF: Hey, you're here now, so…

Take a look

(M *and* G *take a little look around, like potential renters do. They describe a feature or two of the apartment and then, at some point, hold hands while looking.* JEFF, *who was packing a large box with C D binders notices.*)

JEFF: So this must be your second date.

G: Sorry?

JEFF: Never mind. Stupid joke.

[(Pause. The following, if M and G are male:]

[M: That's lesbians.]

[JEFF: Yeah, I'm Stupid, sorry.]

(G *explores more thoroughly.*)

G: Oh, the bathroom's cute
Do you mind if we take pictures?

(While G looks in the bathroom a little, then moves to inspect the bedroom and beyond, M makes a casual effort to continue inspecting the living room. Awkward pause, then)

JEFF: How'd you guys find out about this place?

M: We, uh
We're friends with someone who lives in another building Rogelio manages so he

JEFF: Ah.

M: Have you been here long?

JEFF: Yeah pretty long
Pretty long

(Awkward pause. JEFF goes back to begrudgingly packing.)

JEFF: Can I ask
What's he, uh, asking for, for the rent

M: Uh—

JEFF: Oh, no, I was just *(Curious)*, it's

G: *(From another room)* There's a nice nook here, you could set up your desk
Oh, and this closet! *(Voice diminishing.)* We could totally record in here.

(JEFF stands up.)

JEFF: Oh, you know, I'm thinking of leaving some furniture
(Calling to G) I'm thinking of leaving some furniture if you guys were interested, I could leave them here, or put Post-Its on them if you wanna come back or

G: *(Coming back in. Clearly not interested in the furniture)* Oh, that's awesome.
What do you think, did you look around?

M: Yeah. Did you see everything you wanted

G: I think so. Yeah. And I love the neighborhood—it's nice, right?

JEFF: Oh, it's great.

G: And it's quiet?

JEFF: Real quiet, the walls are thick, the neighbors are nice

G: Oh, thank god. We do a podcast so

M: We need quiet. Our last place

G: Suuuuuucked

JEFF: Well, this is a good apartment. I think you'd be very happy here.
If you, y'know

(M *and* G *look at each other, then turn back to* JEFF.)

M: Do you mind if we ask//

G: Why are you moving?

M: Do you mind if we ask *super abruptly*

G: Sorry, I didn't mean

JEFF: No, it's no problem. No problem. Boring. I got a job. My wife and I are moving to be closer. To the job.

M: Oh!

JEFF: Yeah. I hate to leave this place, but
(*As if it's the farthest place in the world.*) The Bronx

M: Yeesh. Yeah, I bet.

Well, cool—we were just worried it was something like, "This place is haunted," or

G: Screaming fucking assholes outside the window all fucking day like our last place

JEFF: Nope. No problems at all. The water can get a little too hot sometimes, but

M & G: (*Blasé*) Oh noooooo

(They all laugh. Another little awkward beat)

G: *(Quietly, to M)*

I mean, it *is* a little small but

M: We'll talk about it. We gotta go see the other—
(To JEFF*)* Thank you so much, again. For letting
us snoop. Hope you have a great move, yourself!
Congrats on the job.
Are you a D J, by the way? That's a lot of C Ds.

JEFF: No. I just like music.

(Sudden blackout)

Scene Two

(The apartment is now cleared of JEFF*'s stuff. In fact, it's
pretty much cleared of ALL stuff. The room stands empty.
Plastic tarp covers the floor. Perhaps the edges of all the
walls are painted, but not the walls themselves. We hold here
for a moment, then hear a bloodcurdling scream from the
bedroom.)*

G: AAAAAAAAAAAHHHHHHHHHHHHHHHHH
NONONONONONONONONO//NONONONO

(Panicked, M *runs into the living room from the kitchen,
wearing paint clothes and holding a roll of paper towels and
spray cleaner.)*

M: What what what

G: DON'T COME IN HERE

M: What happened

G: Fucking god fuck damn fuck //piece of fuckshit

M: What?!!

G: I dropped the thing

M: What thing?

G: The thing the thing on the ladder, with all the

M: The paint tray?!

G: Yeah…

M: NO

G: Yeah, it mostly landed on the tarp but

M: Honey I love you with all my heart, if you got any paint on my desk I will actually murder you. Like, the real kind. The Scott Peterson kind // or something.

G: I didn't
It's safe
I did, however, get a lot on me

M: That's fine, you're washable.

(Pause)

M: G?

G: I'm coming out now.

(G enters. Covered in paint. G and M stare at each other.)

M: Wow.

G: Shut up.

M: Do I even want to know what it looks like// in there

G: No. Shut up.

M: Here? *(Handing over the paper towels)*

(G tries to wipe off some paint with the towels but it's too tacky. M laughs. G crosses to the bathroom.)

G: *(Genuinely)* Please don't make fun of me, that really wasn't fun

(M peeks into the bedroom. We hear the sound of the sink in the bathroom.)

M: Oh goddddd

G: I just tried to move the ladder like an inch and it folded and the whole thing just
Ugh, and of course now it won't come off! //Grr!

M: You can do it!
But be careful, honey, remember the //water

G: OWWWWW FUCK FUCK

M: Okay *(Begrudgingly rushes to the bathroom now.)*

G: GodDAMN. WHY DOES IT GET SO HOT IT'S LIKE LAVA

M: Do you want some ice

G: NO!!!
(Beat) I don't know, do I?

(M looks in.)

M: Holy crap. This is like a legit first degree burn.
Shit, baby, you're gonna have a blister

G: It's like *boiling water*

M: Do we have butter or //I can go get some burn cream

G: No. We have fucking nothing. *(Exits the bathroom and sits on the tarp on the living room floor)*

G: Let's just move again

M: Okay

G: And we'll just never stop moving. We'll be boxcar hobos but with apartments.

M: Okay

G: How's it going in the kitchen

M: Dude. It is so fucking gross. *(Joining G on the floor)*
There are stains on that floor that I think are even older than me.

(M hugs G.)

G: Don't, you're gonna get paint //on yourself!

M: Shush

(*G and* M *hold each other for a nice moment.*)

G: Speaking of gross

M: The bathroom?

G: Should we flip a coin?

M: I wanna volunteer but I do not want to volunteer

G: Is there, like, bleach downstairs? I can go check.

M: I didn't see any when I was down there.

G: Crap

M: I did see buckets and buckets of industrial adhesive. So maybe, y'know, we can just glue a clean tub into that one.

(*G gets up to look in the bathroom.*)

G: I swear it didn't look like that when we looked at the place

M: Mmmm

G: What do you think it is, rust?

M: Is rust that…browny-reddy?

G: That's exactly what rust-colored means

M: But the water's not like that, like the pipes are clear

G: I have no idea. One more thing for Rogelio.

G & M: Add it to the list!

M: Okay. I'm gonna go take my run to the C V S and get you some burn cream //Yes, I am, yes, I am, it looks nasty

G: Noooooooo
You're nasty

If you see a place that makes keys, don't forget we
need a second set so that I can have keys

M: Okay

G: And beer. Get lots of beer.

M: Okay.

G: And a professional painter. Because we're never
gonna finish painting this place

(M *smacks the wall with a paint-stained hand, leaving a
VERY prominent handprint.*)

M: Now we have to.

G: You are a fucking abomination.

M: You're damn right.

G: Are we stupid for doing this?

M: What, cleaning and painting? //God no

G: No, all of this—leaving, moving here, starting
everything from scratch

M: It's just a different borough

G: Different everything, everything's different

M: We are totally dumb. We are the dumbest. We
are big, dumb dumdums who are dumber than the
dumbest dummy who ever dumbed. But that also
doesn't mean we didn't do the right thing.

G: Aren't you wise

M: NO. But you rest your little blister, and I'll be right
back

G: Okay
Oh! Get some more drop cloths, too, if they have //
any

M: I'M NOT YOUR FUCKING SLAVE

(M *exits, slamming the door. G looks around at the apartment.*)

G: You will be our home, asshole. Heed my words. Okay. Let's fucking do this.

(G *exits into the bedroom. Blackout*)

Scene 3

(*Thunder. The sound of rain outside*)

(*The tarp is gone. Actual furniture pieces are in, including a couch. Boxes. Empty bookshelves. The handprint is still on the wall. M is there, using the voice-to-text iPhone function to write an e-mail.*)

M: "The thing I wish you'd understand-dash-the thing…" (*Doesn't like it. Deletes it.*)
"Let me ask *you* a question-colon-what do you fucking expect from me-question mark."
Ugh. Jesus. No. (*Deletes it.*)

(*The bell buzzes. M goes to the intercom.*)

M: Pablo's House of //Pancakes—

G: Just please let me in

(M *presses the buzzer and cracks the door open. A few moments later, G enters from outside. Wet, shaking off an umbrella and propping it up outside the door*)

(M *puts their phone away guiltily and starts tidying up a bit.*)

M: Hi

G: I got belched on today.

M: What?

(G *struggles to get off rain boots.*)

G: Actually. Belched. On.

My boss decided to come over to my desk, leaned right into my face to look at my monitor, and while she was doing that, just belched. Into my face. No apology. No embarrassment. Just

M: That's disgusting

G: I have to quit, I have to quit, I have to quit

M: Okay, so quit

(G *exits to the bedroom.*)

G: *(Mostly offstage)* Yeah, right.
God, I'm just
If anything sums up what this fucking job is fucking like it's getting belched on. In the face. And there's like a big pile of shit outside, I'm pretty sure it's human shit, it's just everything's great
Hey, my check didn't come, did it?

M: Nope.

G: ARRRRRGH, I'm going to lose my mind. Are you getting mail?

M: I don't really get mail

G: I feel like we're missing most of our mail. Like, I shoulda gotten magazines fucking checks, I renewed my museum membership and I haven't gotten that yet
(*Has exited the bedroom, wearing pajamas, and walks into the kitchen.*)
What should we do for dinner? Should we order something cheap?

M: Honestly? I might pass out soon. I kinda don't care.

(G *pops out of the kitchen, holding two beers.*)

G: You okay?

M: Yeah, just this weather. Hurts.

G: Oh, baby. The…?

M: Yeah. Although, not just that, it just…gets me in a mood, you know?

G: Do you need to talk about //anything

M: No, no

G: Okay.
C'mere

(G *starts kissing* M's *neck.* M *pulls away.*)

M: I can't believe you didn't notice yet

G: Uh-oh, notice what?

M: Did you look in the closet? In the bedroom?

G: Noooo

M: I started putting the sound foamy thingies up

G: You did! Oh, honey, that's great—thank you thank you

M: You're very welcome

G: Something to cross off the list finally! I mean, we still //need to paint this room

M: Shut up, we will.
Also, the piece of resistance.
(*Pulls out a set of keys*)

G: Keys!

M: Keys!

G: Ohmigod I finally have keys!

M: The place was finally open.

G: I want to kiss them but that's gross! Thank fucking Christ!
I still can't believe weird guy only had one set. Didn't he say he had a wife?

M: Yeah, who knows

Given how gross he left this place, his other set
might've just dissolved.

G: Ugh. Still. Yay!
You had a busy day!

M: It's true

(G *and* M *toast. Beat.*)

G: You know I'm gonna ask you about invites next

M: I know. I still don't know why you can't do that, / /
since it's what you do for a living and all

G: Because the last fucking thing I want to do in my
very rare time off is do the same shit that
Okay, okay, I don't want to (*Get into a fight*). Will you
please just
It will help me out immensely and I want us to have a
nice housewarming. Just put the list together, I will do
the rest. Okay?

M: Yeah.

G: It should be super easy, it's not / /like painting

M: I SAID YES, JESUS
Sorry
I'm just not
The rain

G: Okay.

M: I might just lie down for awhile

G: Okay.

(M *heads for the bedroom door. Stops*)

M: He started posting about me again. Michael.

G: Oh.

M: Yup. Calling me a liar and a slut and

G: Ugh

I don't wanna know.

M: I figured.

G: His sick, sad shit, fuck it, it's just air. From an asshole.
It's a fart.

M: I didn't mean to ruin your mood, too, it's just…it's been a day

G: Yeah.
It's okay. Just get some sleep.
How do you know? You still have him blocked all over the place, right? You're not

M: Emily told me.

G: Because you really need to keep him //outta your

M: Emily told me.

G: Emily really shouldn't have.

M: Oh, god, please don't bring it up with her now

G: //Who said I was going to?!

M: I know, you're right. I know. I know. I gotta sleep.

G: Will it bother you if I //turn on the TV or something? I might try to get a little work done. On our business plan.

M: No, no.
Okay. That sounds good.
I'm sorry I'm just kinda done for today.

G: And I'm kinda wired, I got belched on.

M: In the face. It was a big day for both of us.

G: Yeah

M: I love you.

(M closes the door. G starts drinking one of the beers. Lights fade.)

Scene 4

(Several hours later. G is asleep on the couch. It's dark. Really dark. Barely any light at all. There are a few beer bottles on the coffee table.)

(G awakes, confused for a moment. G didn't mean to fall asleep out here and is suitably discombobulated and sore. After a few moments, G looks at his/her phone. When the screen lights up, it becomes apparent that someone is standing in the shadows behind G. G doesn't notice.)

(It's JEFF. He's barely lit, but once we see him, we see him. He watches G.)

(Finally, G gets up and goes to the bedroom. When the door to the bedroom opens, a little moonlight spills into the living room and we see JEFF a little better. He continues to just watch.)

(From the bedroom, we hear M groggily wake up, startled.)

M: Whu?!

G: It's me, baby. Sorry. Stay sleeping.

M: I was having the dream again. Bad dream // red
Red

G: Shhh. I'm here.

(JEFF sits on the couch and just continues staring after them. He also takes in the new room, the furniture, the arrangement.)

(Perhaps G closes the door and the lighting change takes us to black. Or we just watch JEFF for a few moments and fade out.)

Scene 5

(Hey, the apartment looks great! Tidied up. Furniture rearranged for maximum efficiency. Perhaps even some more chairs added. The wall, unsurprisingly, is still unpainted, save for the one handprint.)

(M and G call to each other from separate rooms, both offstage.)

G: What about music?

M: What?

G: WHAT ABOUT MUSIC
(Enters the living room)

M: OH I MADE A PLAYLIST IT'S REALLY GOOD IT STARTS WITH D'ANGELO AND THEN PRINCE AND THEN SOME MORE D'ANGELO

G: Great, it's a housewarming, it's not an orgy

M: Not with that attitude, dumdum
(Enters with a little handmade sign)

G: Bathroom's all set, kitchen's all set. God, we are never going to paint this room, are we

M: I made a sign.
(Shows the sign. It reads, in large but hip letters, "WARNING: LAVA")

G: No one is going to have any clue what that means

M: Desiree always tries to do dishes. She has to be warned. And I can make another one for the bathroom. How are we doing on snacks.

G: Oh, we are good to go on snacks, my friend. Peanut-free, soy-free, gluten-free, dairy-free, sugar-free, fucking-molecule-free. And for the fully functioning humans, I've got deep fried edamame mozzarella sticks with an almond dipping sauce.

M: You are a god[dess]

G: I have been telling you this for years

M: We should get you a scroll or a // banner

G: Hey

M: What?

G: I love you

(G *and* M *kiss. Deeply and tenderly. Then hold each other in their new home.*)

G: More of that here, please. I want this place to have more of that.

M: Agreed.

(G *and* M *disengage and go back to prepping for the party.*)

G: Can I…run something by you?

M: What?

G: This is gonna sound weird but…I've just been thinking//…since you brought it up a couple weeks ago

M: Uh-oh
What?

G: Well
You know the other night when we heard someone in the garbage
Or, like, our mail problems
Or people ringing our bell at random times
You don't think it's…

M: …what, Berit?

G: Fucking with us? Do you think it's possible

M: Berit doesn't know where we live

G: But friends do. Friends of friends.

M: This is kinda out of //left field, baby

G: I know, just been thinking.
This is a big deal, this party, it's like we're, I dunno,
coming out again almost. We haven't hosted
something together since The Incident. We're in a new
borough. It's

M: I highly doubt any friends of ours would tell Berit
where we're living

G: Me, too. But if Michael's been posting again, I
dunno
(*Beat*)
I just don't know what the two of them are capable //
of

(*There's a knock on the apartment door. G and M both jump.
Beat*)

G: It's waaaaay too early

M: Yeah, not for Stephanie
Can we—just—put a pin in that thought

G: Yeah
Sorry, I didn't mean to—forget it

(*G and M go to the door and open it. It's* JEFF.)

JEFF: Howdy!

M: Oh!

G: Jesus
Hi! What an unexpected

JEFF: Is this a bad time?

M: Uh

G: No, I mean, maybe
We have some people coming over in a…
In a few minutes

JEFF: Oh wow!

(*They stare at each other awkwardly.*)

G: What's up?   M: Do you want to come
                                 in?

JEFF: …I mean, if you don't mind? It'd be fun to see
what you've done to the place

(G *and* M *move aside and let* JEFF *in. He admires the*
changes.)

JEFF: Niiiiiiice
You guys have really
Really changed it up
(*He's staring at the handprint on the wall.*)

G: So, what can we do for you?

JEFF: Oh, ha! Right. Sorry.
I was actually just in the area, thought I'd come by and
see if I've gotten any mail. I feel like I'm missing a lot
of mail at my new place. //You know the Post Office.

M: Oh

G: Oh!
Dude. I have been missing big ol' chunks of mail for
weeks now, too! Is this like a normal thing here?

JEFF: Not usually, no—there might be a new guy, or, or
girl, I dunno. Crap.

G: Yeah, I've got a bunch of paychecks missing

M: Magazines

G: I'm waiting on a museum membership card

JEFF: (*Practically in one breath*) Oh! There is an *amazing*
exhibit at the Natural History Museum right now,
about the Japanese Giant Hornet, you ever heard about
the Japanese Giant Hornet? They're actually one of the
leading causes of death in Japan. Big as your thumb.
And it actually spits, or shoots, I dunno, this acidic
venom from its tail end, where it's also got this huge
stinger. They have videos of what, like, seven of them

can do to a whole colony of European honeybees. They just massacre like fifty thousand bees without breaking a sweat. It's, it's just astounding.

(Beat)

M: I didn't know hornets could sweat.

JEFF: I
Am an idiot. Sorry. I'll get out of your hair. Just, if you get anything

M: We'll hold onto it for you

JEFF: Awesome. I promise not to come back and bug you much—ha, bug—I'm just waiting on a couple important things, so of course

G: Of course

(JEFF starts to make his way back to the door.)

JEFF: Have a good, is it a housewarming?

G: Yeah

JEFF: Noice. Noice. You guys have a lot of friends in the neighborhood already or?

M: Uh, we know some people here already
And some more are just hopping on a train

JEFF: Like college friends or?
(Awkward beat)
(Embarrassed) Sorry, I'm just always curious how friends meet. I don't make friends. I'm being an idiot, //I'll

M & G: *(Embarrassed, as well)* No, no, no

(It's painfully obvious how lonely JEFF is.)

G: Uh
Well, I know Chris from college

M: Yeah, and I met his girlfriend,// where? Oh, "wife"

G: Wife

It was while you were bartending

M: No, no, it was before that, wasn't it, //because
that's how I got the job

G: No, I don't—oh, yeah
Shit. It's all a blur.
We used to run in a very weird circle, //it was kind of
a performance commune, cabarets and

M: Intense, intense circle

G: We were pretty wild

M: To be honest, I barely remember most if it, we got
fucked //up a lot

G: Speak for yourself, I remember

M: Well, and not anymore, I'm a total lightweight now
But that's kinda what our podcast, we're curating a
podcast, it's kinda half storytelling, half roundtable,
about mistakes—poking fun at
I'm no good at //pitching it, that's what G does

Jeff: I don't
What's a podcast?

M: Oh, it's like

G: Internet radio

M: On demand

Jeff: Cool

M: Yeah

Jeff: Well, you guys should interview me sometime,
my life has been
Pretty interesting.
Hahahaha

(Beat)

G: Are you heading back to the Bronx?

JEFF: *(A very subtle realization)* Yes, yeah
Heading back to the Bronx

G: I mean, we hate to kick you out

M: This is also kind of an official meeting

G: Kind of an investment thing
Housewarming-slash-investment pitch thing

JEFF: You guys are looking for investors?

M: Podcasts ain't cheap, you gotta buy bandwidth and
//equipment and

G: Okay

JEFF: I'd love to invest. If you need investors.

M: Uh

JEFF: Yeah, just came into some money, actually, and I
have no idea what to do with it, so

(Beat)

G: Really?

JEFF: Yeah. My mom just died

M: Oh, I'm so sorry

JEFF: *(Shrugging)* Cha-ching, right?
I mean, it wasn't soon enough to let me keep this place
but
I'd love to throw in some dollars, y'know?
Some bucks.
(Beat)
Some shekels.
(Beat)
I could even run to our little liquor store and get some
hooch! For the par-tay!

(M and G look at each other, miserable. Blackout)

Scene 6

(Music underneath: M's sexy playlist. Special on JEFF, *holding a wine glass, as he gives a toast.)*

JEFF: Hey, everyone, can I
I just wanted to take a sec
(To M *and* G*)*
Happy Warm House. Welcome to the neighborhood.
This is a really great neighborhood. I have lived here a
long time. And, y'know, this world is, is a cold, deep
crater of shit. But not with people like M and G. They
have moved here and, and
I'm just so happy.
Um
There is an exhibit at the museum right now, it's
amazing, all about
There's this hornet, the Japanese giant hornet, big
as my thumb! Spits poison! Horrifying! And, and
that's the kind of world we live in, guys. And these
hornets, they can massacre entire colonies of European
honeybees, right? M and G? You know this, right?
They just slice them in half with their jaws like an
assembly line until the ground is literally carpeted.
But that's the European honeybees. The *Japanese*
honeybees…this is their *home*. They know how to
protect their hive, they know, because
So, when the hornets, when they send a scout out to
look for beehives, the Japanese honeybees all know to
hide. To draw the hornet inside, and then what they
all know to do next is amazing, they all land on top of
the hornet, all of them, and they start rubbing their legs
together. They can't pierce his armor, they know this,
and you can see em, they do thermal imaging of them.
They immobilize the intruder…and then they cook it.
Roast it. To death. Within like one degree of their own
lives. And isn't that incredible?

Home
Is a very important thing. A strengthening thing. When you're home, you can do anything.
So to M and G: welcome home.

Scene 7

(M and G are in the middle of a long, tiring fight. There's a large suitcase in the living room.)

G: *(So over it)* Can I just explain what I'm trying

M: *(Ditto)* You can try

G: Because I really don't want to keep fighting right // before I leave

M: I'm not the one trying to fight

(G's cellphone rings. G and M both groan. G looks at it.)

G: Fuck. It's Chris. It'll be quick—//can we

M: *(Almost to self)* No, great. I guess I'll just…keep fucking working or something

G: Take a break, hang on

(G answers the phone while M goes into the bedroom.)

G: *(Very cheery)* Hey!
Yeah, no, you just caught me. I'm heading to the airport in like an hour
Two fucking weeks.
Yeah, it's *insane*, but—need the money. What's up?

(From the bedroom:)

M: GODDAMMIT

G: *(Still on the phone)* Right.
Oh, coooooool.
Yes, absolutely, tell him we'd love to talk.
Well, we *kiiinda* have something

(M *storms out of the bedroom, holding some sound-insulating foam, seething. The foam gets tossed on the couch.*)

G: (*On the phone, concurrent with below*) We tried recording a, a test episode, like a pilot, but the sound was weird, we have to reconfigure the acoustic tiling and maybe get, I think, a preamp for the microphone. It sounds kinda shitty. So I'd love to hold off on sending him something if you think he'd be willing to wait.

M: (*Concurrent with above*) Fucking things fucking don't wanna fucking move I have to fucking rip them fucking out of the fucking wall and I don't fucking know how I'm gonna fucking get them back fucking up again it's a fucking waste of fucking money

(M *storms out of the apartment and slams the door.*)

G: Yeah, sorry. It's just a little tense here.
Well, yeah, 'cause of the episode and…other things.
No, no, no.
But you think he'd wait for us? Or should we just send him the shitty scratch demo? We can try to redo everything as soon as humanly
Uh-huh
Uh-huh

(*There's a noise outside. G peeks out while listening.*)

G: Hey, lemme ask you something, do you know if Desiree or Stephanie are still talking to Berit?
No, no reason. Just wanna make sure there are no unwelcome run-ins.
Yeah
(*Re* JEFF) Oh shit, I know, THAT guy. No, he used to live here, he just came by and
I don't know, dude. He's a little, uh, little offputting, right? I mean, he says he wants to invest but—

Oh god no, I don't think we could ever take him up on it. He's a bit much.

(M *comes back into the apartment, carrying a very heavy drum of industrial adhesive. Like a large bucket of paint. It's clearly difficult to carry it.* M *drops it in the living room, rests, then prepares to try to carry it to the bedroom.*)

G: *(Whispering, to M)* What are you doing?

M: *(Struggling; so mad)* Don't, just

G: *(On the phone)* Ha! Yeah, no shit, hey, Chris, can I maybe call you right back?
Or//
Okay, even better. Yeah, tell him we'll have something for him in two weeks. And if you think he's getting antsy, lemme know ASAP.

M: No. Don't. Have your happy little chat with Chris.

G: *(Phone)* Awesome. Thank you so much for playing go-between. I owe you many beers. I'll try. Bye! Muah. *(Hangs up. Immediately; to M)* What the fuck are you doing?

M: The pads aren't going back up easily so I'm going to use this shit from the basement

G: Okay but why are you doing this now, //we're talking

M: Didn't stop you from getting on the phone

G: Let's please not keep fighting. Come on, stop, you're gonna hurt yourself

M: It's gotta get done, G, I'd love to not do it, but you're going away so //I'm kinda stuck

G: God, now you're gonna punish me for having to work? I have to work! I would love not to have to work!

M: Spending all this fucking money, we coulda produced like two cabarets already

G: Yeah, that's worked out so well for us so far.

M: And I would love to be able to work, don't throw that in my face

G: Why are you being so fucking venomous right now?

M: I told you something—in confidence—as my partner—and you fucking judged me for it

G: I wasn't judging! I just didn't like that you lied to me. //Yes you did.

M: I did not lie. All I fucking said was I was thinking, *thinking* about getting in touch // with him.

G: You told me you'd completely cut him off, and now you're telling me you're up to date with every little thing he's saying online! This piece of shit who is obsessed with defending someone who did something horrific to you! I'm not judging! I'm just…scared for you.

M: I don't need you to be scared for me, // I can do that fine on my own. And I'm the one who paid the price, I got the shit beaten out of me, so maybe let me feel the things I need to feel and stop getting in the way of my, my

G: I just don't want to see you get sucked back into that shit and get hurt again, it's awful, and you're right, I'm sorry I hate seeing you hurt and I just want us to be done with that part of our lives so let's just fucking get married okay will you marry me

(Beat. That was unexpected. This all tumbles out.)

M: What.

G: I know, it just came out of my mouth

M: You

G: I know

M: You always said you never wanted to get married

G: Yeah, but I think that's because we never could and and all the shit with Berit happened and we had to figure life out and

M: Now

G: I don't know! I don't know! You're trying to glue foam squares to a wall and it's for our new life together and it's really sexy and beautiful and I don't know I just really want us stop feeling like we're in hiding and throw a party and sign a contract that says we'll do this until we're dead

M: ...are you gonna pull out a // ring?

G: NO I DON'T HAVE A RING this is happening completely unexpectedly!

M: You *plan events* for a living—you're really bad at planning events!

G: Look, are you going to answer //the fucking question or not, M, shut the fuck

M: You didn't pose it as a question, you just stated it and of course.
Of course I'll marry you.

G: Okay! Good!

(G *and* M *kiss again, more passionately this time.*)

G: I guess we'll talk about it more when I get back? I mean, we'll talk while I'm gone but

M: Okay

G: And I'm sorry if it sounds like I want to protect you. I mean, I do, but I know you don't *need* it, you know, I know //you can take care of yourself

M: Okay. Time to shut the fuck up.

(M *looks at the bedroom, then starts to pull* G *into it.*)

G: I'm sorry I took Chris's call

M: Shut the fuck up

G: But he might be able to get us sponsorship

M: Shut the fuck up

G: For the podcast

M: Shut the fuck up

G: And I should probably leave for the airport

M: Shut the fuck up

G: Because my plane leaves in like two hours

M: Shut the fuck up

G: But I'll be home in two weeks

M: Shut the fuck up

(G *and* M *disappear into the bedroom. Diligent audience members will notice* JEFF *barely visible outside the living room window, looking in.*)

Scene 8

(*The apartment is empty. The suitcase is gone. There are a couple more tubs of the industrial adhesive by the door. Regular ambient noise for a sunny afternoon.*)

(*After a few moments,* JEFF *enters from the kitchen, talking to someone in the bedroom.*)

JEFF: Oh, there's also this Indian place called Tagine, uh, Palace, I think—have you guys tried that yet? Like ten blocks away? Not too spicy, thank God. Sometimes Indian can just wreck my stomach, you know? Nobody wants to be around that! Ha!

Did

Did you fall asleep in there?

(There's no answer. JEFF *goes about moving some furniture around in the living room, humming to himself. Then he stops, almost guiltily.)*

JEFF: Hey, look

I appreciate you being so understanding. About the sleeping arrangements. The salesguy told me those cots are super comfy, the comfiest they've got. I'm sure it doesn't compare to the bed, but.

I just figured you'd like the option to change rooms, move around a bit. Couldn't do that if—

(He peeks into the bedroom.)

Oh, you're totally awake! Howdy! You wanna come out into the living room? Yeah, come on out!

*(*JEFF *steps into the bedroom, then comes back out, pushing a cot on wheels. M is lying on top of it. Every inch of M's flesh is shiny and seamed with gunk. M has been glued to the cot. It looks horrifying, almost insectile, and it's apparent from M's complete lack of movement that the bond is unbelievably strong. Perhaps the head of the cot is able to be folded up a bit so that M isn't lying completely flat. When the cot's in place, he locks the wheels.)*

JEFF: I moved stuff around, hope you don't mind. Not that that stopped you guys!

What do you think, Indian?

Well?

Hey.

M: I'm not hungry

JEFF: Nah, you gotta eat. You were *out cold.* You gotta bounce back from that. Get your strength!

(M starts trying to struggle, barely succeeding in rocking the cot a little.)

JEFF: Oooo, no, no, no, not like that! Hey. Shhh. Don't do that, seriously. I don't know if you'd survive the,

the ripping, if you did. It'd take off your whole…
everything.

This glue is intense! I mean, you shoulda seen me, I
was so scared of getting any on me! Ha!

Sorry. That's really kinda insensitive of me.

M: I think some of my hair is caught

JEFF: Ohhhhhh, shoot. That really sucks. I'm sorry
*(He does nothing to help. He continues moving stuff
around.)*

Okay. Well, I'm gonna get Indian, then. And I will
get you, I dunno, something soft, some chicken tikka?
Unless you're a vegan, which is totally cool. Speak now
or forever hold your peas and carrots. Heh.

M: What are you going to do to me?

JEFF: *(Almost nicely)* Do you know who Procrustes is?
He was a guy Theseus defeated, back in the Greeky
times. My parents used to love to read me that stuff.
Anytime someone would come over to *his house*, he
didn't like intruders, so he'd have them lie on this bed.
And if they were too small, he'd tie them to a rack and
stretch them until they fit. If they were too big, he'd
chop off legs or feet, to make 'em fit. I guess we all deal
with houseguests differently.

I'm not gonna do anything to you. We're gonna have
some food and then maybe…redecorate a little. Re-
redecorate. Hahaha.

Oh, man. Good to be home!

(Lights fade)

Scene 9

(M *has been left out in the living room. Light from the*
windows indicates time has passed. M *desperately tries to*
move, but it's no use. M *strains against the bond and barely*
moves a centimeter. Tries again. Nothing. Out of breath
now.)

(*Meanwhile, there's a rustling in the kitchen: furniture*
being moved, grunts from JEFF. *Then, from the bedroom, the*
hum of a cellphone on vibrate. M *hears it—it's* M's *phone.*
A look of longing crosses M's *face. And maybe the first*
semblance of a plan. The phone continues to ring until it
goes to voicemail.)

(*From the kitchen:)*

JEFF: (*Offstage)* But seriously, this table…is so much
better…over here! You're right by the window, you can
have coffee while you watch the sunrise! It's so much
better it's insane! Hahaha.

(*While he speaks he comes into the living room and plops*
down on the couch. Maybe he's eating takeout.)

Speaking of insane, I can't *believe* you guys didn't want
that shelving unit I had in there! Like, where were you
gonna put pots, ya loonies?! Now we're gonna have
to go and find another one and I don't even remember
where I got it in the first place! Mighta been on the
street, actually. You can't always trust street stuff,
but this neighborhood's actually pretty reliable, good
people. I mean there are always exceptions but.
Is there anything scarier than bed bugs? I don't think
so!

(*The phone in the bedroom starts vibrating.* JEFF *hears the*
faint buzzing.)

JEFF: What is that?
You hear that?
Like a

Don't get up.
(He looks around for the source, heads into the bedroom.
Offstage)
Well, ho-leee crap
(He comes back in holding M's phone, laughing.)
This
On the floor by the bed! How did I miss this??
"Dumdum" was calling, is that G? That's cute.
If you want, you can gimme your password, I can tell
you what s/he said.
(Beat)
No? You don't wanna know?
Okayyyyyyy.
(He puts it in his pocket. He sits back down.)
So, she[he]'s gone for a work thing, right? She[He]
does, like, party planning? Is that freelance, or does she
work with, like, a company? The ol' Dance of the 1099s.
Is this normal, going out of town for, for work? That
must get pretty lonely. For both of you.
Not that there's anything wrong with…with being
lonely.
(The handprint on the wall catches his eye. He tries to ignore
it for a second, but gets up and looks at it.)
Ugh. There's gonna be a lot to do in this room
This is—why would you just deface a space like this, I
I can't think about it too much, I'll start getting upset.
Do you know, when I first moved in here, there was
wallpaper on this wall? Can you believe it? Really
gnarly stuff. I had to peel it all off and then rub down
the walls. That took. A. While. But it was worth it,
don't you think?
Yeah.
How are you? Are you comfortable? More or less.

M: *(Firm; oddly not scared)* Please let me go. Please. You have to stop this.

JEFF: *(Smiling; this is fun)* Ohh, okay. *This* again.

(At the same time:)

M: Why are—	JEFF: *(Predicting)* "Why a are you doing this?"
(Pause)	
Please—	"Please"
(Pause)	
Stop—	"Stop"
(Pause)	
I have to go to the bathroom	"I—"
	Oh

(JEFF stares at M for a few beats. He hadn't considered this.)

JEFF: You have to go
To the bathroom

M: Yes

JEFF: Oh. Uh.
Like right now?

M: Yes.

JEFF: I
I didn't think of that
Can it, can it wait

M: I don't know

(Pause)

JEFF: I guess we could, uh, tilt you up against the, in the bathroom against the wall, or
I don't suppose you can lift

M: I can't, it's—

JEFF: —all over your backside, I know.
Huh.

Well, this was dumb of me. Heh. Ohhhhhhh boy. The
bathroom!
*(He laughs, shaking his head, and walks into the kitchen. He
comes back in with a box. Aimless. Puts it on the couch. It
becomes very apparent that he's upset and trying to cover.)*

M: Have you never…done this before?

JEFF: I mean, I don't know, I guess we could set a towel
down or, or, or, I dunno, hang air fresheners from
(Picks the box back up)
Air fresheners, right, great idea, you wanna live like
that? That's a brilliant fucking idea, dipshit.
Um
Jeez, what am I holding this *(Box)*, I'm all, I'm all
scatterbrained now
And
And
*(He throws the box against the wall. Its contents scatter and
break. To himself; whispered, almost embarrassed)*
See?! This is why! This is why! You fucking moron! //
This is why, you, you dolt, you idiot!

M: Hey. Stop. // Hey, it's okay

JEFF: You forget to check for a phone, you forget to
plan for bathroom stuff, you are so. Goddamn. Useless!
God! Dammit!

M: HEY
I can hold it! I'll just hold it!

JEFF: What

M: I will just…hold it
You, just, take a breath and, and we'll…figure out what
you need to do
It's okay. I'm okay. Just take a breath

*(JEFF tries to take M's advice and takes an almost comically
large inhale/exhale.)*

JEFF: Okay. You're right.

Thanks roomie.

Okay. Okay

This still doesn't feel right, though.

This still

Ohhhhhhhhhhhhhhh holy crap

(He storms into the bedroom. Then, JEFF *practically skips out of the bedroom, dressed to leave. A man on a mission. He speaks as he moves, never stopping. Giddy, excited)*

I know what'll help, // I know what'll help, I know what'll help!

M: No, no, wait!

*(*JEFF *exits the apartment. The door slams behind him. M is left all alone.)*

(M moans. Long pause. M tries even harder to escape. No luck.)

M: Okay

Okay

Okay

AAAAAAAAAHHHHHHHHH

(Lights fade.)

Scene 10

(It's night now. The apartment is pretty dark. M is still where JEFF *left the cot, but seems to have passed out. The sound of keys, the front door opens. Red light from the hallway pours into the apartment.)*

M: *(Waking, blearily)* Baby is that you?

(A sound of rushing air turns into a creature's growl… which immediately cuts out when JEFF *enters, holding a box, a plastic shopping bag around his wrist. As he speaks*

he gently puts the box down—it's something heavy and precious. The light has gone back to normal.)

JEFF: Ugh! Hardware store was closed, had to hop on a train and find a Home Depot. Ugh! Such a waste of a day! Oh, boy.
Did you scream a lot?

M: What?

JEFF: While I was gone? Did you scream a lot?

M: Yeah.

JEFF: But no one came over?

M: No

JEFF: These walls, man. Solid. Prewar!
(He strokes the wall, practically hugs it. Sighs, lovingly.)
Oh well, can't says I blame you.
(He goes to the bedroom. Offstage)
So, I have a surprise for you, I think you're gonna like it
(Comes back with a C D binder)
When I first moved here—this was a looong time ago—that hardware store was one of the only things around. Times, they have a-changed.
Where are you from, by the way?

M: …Ohio

JEFF: Ohio! Ooo. Exotic.
(He opens up the box he brought in and pulls out a small-ish stereo system and speakers. Something about this system looks very personal—stickers or something.)

M: You got that at Home Depot?

JEFF: *("Duh")* No, no, all this was in the basement, where I've been living.
(He sets up the speakers.)
Anyway

Where *I* grew up, I had a pretty awful time. Both
my parents were dead, I never got to meet them—I
bounced in and out of foster homes and, and, *other*
places. I'd wake up and not know where I was. "Where
am I? This isn't my home." Panic would set in. It's a
horrible feeling.
And it got even worse when I moved to this city.
This is what I got at Home Depot
(He goes to the shopping bag and pulls out a putty knife.)
This should cut through some of the glue, right? //I
can't promise it won't hurt like the Dickens but

M: Oh god! Thank you. Thank you

JEFF: That is the weirdest phrase, have you ever
thought about that? Where does that come from?
I wonder—hahaha—I wonder if, if, if someone got hit
with a, a, book of his once, one of the big ones. Like,
"Ow!" But then he got hurt again later and was like,
"That hurt almost as bad as the Dickens you threw at
me!" Hahaha!
(He can barely control himself, laughing. After a beat)
No, probably not.
I also got these! *(He pulls out wee-wee pads from the bag.)*
We can just slide 'em under you and voila.
Give me a letter.

M: What?

JEFF: A letter. A part of the alphabet.

M: Why?

JEFF: Hmm, no, name another one.

M: …G

JEFF: Perfect! *(He heads over to his C D binder.)* Let's see
what we've got in—aww, that's sweet, "G," I just got
that. *(Flips through pages in the binder)* Okay. Yeah, why
not.

(As he speaks, he pulls out a C D and puts it in the stereo system. Takes the C D to the right track. Continuous) Anyway, the reason I say it was worse when I moved here was, before I found this place, I bounced around neighborhoods and apartments and each one seemed like it was going to work out, but somehow they always wound up being worse than the last one. That made it harder. Like they were lying to me. But, so I used to wander around, looking for somewhere to, to, be, until I found these special kinds of bars. And I would stay there all night, because even though I had a home…it wasn't the right home.

This is my favorite thing. It's how I relax and have fun. And it'll keep me focused while I *(Wiggles the knife)* work on you. Try to hold still. And join in if you want!

(JEFF presses play. A loud karaoke version of something recognizable and beginning with the letter G begins to play. The reason I'm keeping it vague is because just in case any production ever meets with any copyright problems, you can easily change the track night by night. Clever, right? Insidious. Just for now, let's say it's something from Grease. "Summer Nights," maybe.)

(JEFF dances a bit to the music, getting closer to M. When he sings, he uses the putty knife as a microphone. But here's the thing. He doesn't sing the lyrics to this song. He sings the lyrics to a different song. Any other song you want. Let's Stay Together. I Got You Babe. Whatever. And he doesn't try to fit the lyrics into the musical phrasing—he's literally just singing a different song over the karaoke backing track. The effect should be disorienting and weird.)

(His voice is also bizarre. Operatic or dance-hall-y. Out of time and place. Tone-deaf. Nothing he does fits.)

M: Those aren't the words—

(JEFF sings louder, smiling broadly. M can't take it.)

M: Those aren't the words!

JEFF: (*Loving it*) I KNOW! *Dumdum!*
All my life, I never quite fit in. Anywhere. At home,
at school. This is my little way of saying, y'know,
"screw fitting in!" Right? It's Jeff-eoke! You try it! Sing
something.

(JEFF *stares at* M *until* M *sings.* M *sings the right words.*)

JEFF: No! No, you gotta sing something *different*!

(JEFF *stares at* M *again. Then he shows* M *the knife as a
reminder.* M *starts to sing something different. "Jingle
Bells" or something equally innocuous. He joins in with* M,
then takes over singing. He gets closer to M. *He starts to cut
away at the glue under* M's *upper thighs and crotch.* M *is
suitably uncomfortable and scared. And it hurts.*)

M: STOP
STOP

(JEFF *abruptly pulls his hand away. Disgusted and furious*)

JEFF: Oh God, you pissed on my hand
You pissed on my hand
What do I do, what do I

(JEFF *drops the knife and storms over to the stereo and tries
to turn it off without touching it. Then he runs into the
bathroom.* M *squirms, able to lift his/her/their hips up from
the cot. It's not much…but it's a start.*)

M: (*Realizing s/he can move a little*) Oh god…oh god

(*From the bathroom, the water is running:*)

JEFF: (*Offstage*) Ew. Ew. Ew.
(*Then, suddenly:*) OW!!!!!!!!
OWWW!
(*He comes back in, wiping his hands on his pants. He's so
furious he can barely stand it.*)
I forgot how hot the water gets.

M: I'm sorry

JEFF: I can't. Believe. I forgot. How Hot. The water gets.

M: // I'm sorry.

JEFF: Okay, we have to talk. And I'm sorry if I get
upset, I'm really trying to be as, as, as even-tempered
as I can be, but
HOUSE MEETING, that's what people say, right?
This whole situation.
I don't normally do this, okay? Have roommates, I
mean. I'm a solitary guy. I like my solitartyness. My
solitude, that's it. I like to be alone. So I have dealt
with intruders, I have dealt with people who have
overstayed their welcome. Because I like. To be. Alone.
And then…I was told I had to leave. My home. And if
you like to be alone, that's like being told you have to
leave yourself. I don't want to do that, I like myself.
So I was prepared to just *deal* with you, whoever you
were, make you disappear and move back in, but
then…I saw you and G. You guys were so together and
lovely and, I don't know. For the first time I realized
that maybe I wasn't alone. Maybe what I was was
lonely.
I mean, I *work*, I see the world, but you know it's not
the same. Maybe it's not healthy to coop up at home by
yourself.
So, I dunno, I guess I wanted to try to share my home
with someone. With you. "You should always be ready
to let go of things." My dad used to tell me that. Maybe
solitaryness is one of those things you should give up.

M: Solitude

JEFF: BUT I'm also realizing I might not be mentally
prepared to take on a roommate. There's so many
logistics to consider and, and, I keep seeing things
you guys changed around and that's, like, viscerally
upsetting to me. That *frgnn* hand is, like, waving to me,
"Hi, look at me!"

And to make everything a BAJILLION times worse…I just forget how hot the water gets. In my own home. So…I don't know, M, the only solution I keep coming back to…is glue. Because when the hornet arrives, you gotta immobilize it. Before it takes over your home.

M: It's not your home anymore, it's // our home

JEFF: DO YOU REALLY THINK THAT'S THE BEST THING TO SAY TO ME RIGHT NOW
(He goes to a bucket of adhesive and picks up a paintbrush sitting on top of the lid.)
This makes me super uncomfortable! But you need to pay the price!
For every change you've made to this house, you get more glue. Let's say all *this (He gestures to the glue already covering M)* takes care of, of the furniture and, and that awful, awful handprint. But it's time for some more.
Where do you want it?
And, and you don't get to say, like, "My belly button" or something DUMB. It's gotta be uncomfortable. Because not having a home is uncomfortable. *Being gone so long you forget how hot the water can get is uncomfortable.*
So, please. Tell me where.
Your mouth?
An eye?
An ear?
Your nostril? You could still breathe, just…
You gotta be willing to let go of things, M! What do you want to lose?
What if I glue *that* shut *(Pointing to M's crotch)*? That'd take care of our bathroom problem, right?
PICK A FUCKING PART ALREADY YOU FUCKING HORNET COME ON

(At JEFF's *yelling, something in* M *kind of turns off.* M *retreats, mentally.)*

M: *(Quietly)* I don't care. Do whatever you want. Just stop yelling

JEFF: I don't want to decide!!!
(Finally, he makes a whining noise.) Fine! How about your...left ear. That seems harmless enough.
But for every change in the apartment I find, we're gonna need to pick somewhere else.
(He goes back over to the tub of adhesive, opens it, and dips the paintbrush in. As he does so:)
Yeah. I guess that's like a Buddhist thing or a zen thing or something, right? "Let go of attachments." My dad was a smart guy. My mom died when I was very little and he raised me all by himself, no rulebook, no advice. Just him and me. And every day I try to be like him.
I mean, not in *all* respects but

M: Wait, I thought you said you never knew your parents
Or that your mom *just* died

(Beat)

JEFF: I
Wait
(He absently grabs one of his earlobes.)
I
(A barely audible whisper) I don't want to talk about that

*(*JEFF *stops and stares into space for a few moments, holding his earlobe. He puts the brush down, goes to the stereo. He pulls out a C D, puts it in. Presses play. Weird, sad karaoke music fills the room.)*

(Then, without a word or ceremony, he exits to the bedroom and closes the door.)

(M watches him go, confused.)

(The distant sound of thunder.)

M: Great.

(Starts to lift themself off of the cot some more. Peeling more adhesive away, bit by bit. It hurts. But M's making progress.)

Scene 11

(The music becomes the distant sound of a party down a hallway in another room. On another part of the stage, a special hits G, who is pacing and speaking into a cellphone.)

G: Sometimes you have nightmares

(The lights on M begin to fade. M, of course, doesn't hear any of this.)

G: It's a little after midnight. I'm in a hotel room in Redondo. I can't sleep, partly because someone is throwing one hell of a party down the hall, and partly because if I have to think about our fucking client's fifth amendment to the twelfth redraft of his stupid bullshit app launch party extravaganza bullshit anymore, I'm going to peel off my face with an oyster fork and go around slapping people with it. Seriously, I wonder if people know that when you say you're an event planner, what you actually mean is you just adopt the shittiest children in the world for a few weeks at a time and let them throw feces at you. Anyway. Since I know I need to get better at just talking and, uh, speaking into a microphone (good job so far), I've decided to record this very special episode of the M&G Podcast. I'm recording it onto my phone so the sound quality is going to be for shit, but that's okay, we're not going to release it. This episode is just for you. My love.

It's raining where you are. I checked the weather after
I tried calling and texting all day and haven't gotten
a response. I think you're doing that thing you do
sometimes where you…disappear for a little while.
Uh, I'm gonna be totally honest with you, I have
absolutely no idea how to deal with you when you do
this. I don't want to smother you or baby you, and it
does drive me a little insane that you won't let me, I
dunno, help somehow.
But I hope you also know
I don't ever want you to feel like you have to change. I
want me to be the one to change and, and learn. I hope
you know that it's okay and that I understand that you
need to go through what you need to go through to
heal. If that makes any sense.

Because I also know you have nightmares sometimes.

(G *pauses, anxious. The sound of the party outside are faint
but audible.*)

G: Jeez, they're really going out there.
It's all I can do right now to not run out of this hotel,
hop on a plane, and come home to you.
I want to run and make sure you're okay right now.
Which is really fucking stupid. A) because I would lose
my job and have to pay back a gignatic retainer. But
also B) of course you're okay.
You are the fucking strongest person I have ever met,
M. When I think of all the things you've had to go
through. All the things you've survived.
Sometimes I want to yell at other people, "Do you
know who you're fucking talking to, what this
amazing person has been through? Do you have any
idea what it would be like as a fucking 13 year old to,
to fucking discover the bodies when her brother shot
their mom and then killed himself? Do you know this
person fucking held her father's hand while he was

dying of fucking awful fuck cancer four years later? Do
you know what she fucking survived *last year*?
And you're mad because she got into the wrong line
at C V S?! You imaginary person I'm yelling at right
now?!" I want to, to physically break every person who
doesn't bow down to you sometimes.
I mean, obviously I don't. I know I can be a cunt
sometimes, but, shit, it's my instinct to hide in a closet
anytime something gets scary or, or confrontational.
Ever since I was a little kid, anytime my parents
got into a fight, they knew exactly where to find me
afterwards. They didn't even have to search, they just
went straight for the
You're not like that. Whether you know it or not. And
here's the point of this Very Special Episode I'm going
to secretly upload onto your phone next time you're in
the shower or something. And I'm gonna call it "For
your next rainy day".
You have nightmares sometimes.
I think about your nightmares a lot, I mean the regular
one, the frequent one you have sometimes. I kinda
reenact it in my head. A lot.
You're alone. You're walking through the woods or
an empty building. And you know the thing is coming
for you. The red thing. You don't know what it is, but
you can sense its malevolence. Its...*redness*. Coming
towards you. So you run. Of course you run, it's a
nightmare. And because it's a nightmare, it follows.
No matter where you turn or hide, it gets closer...and
closer.
And this is the thing I love about you so much. Even
though I know it's the worst part. Even though I know
it terrifies you.
The red thing catches you.
(Starting to have a panic attack)
The red thing catches you.

Sometimes you wake up and you can't move, you can't
make a sound. I'm awake, too, I'm right next to you
and I can tell what's happening. I know the red thing
has caught you. You're drowning in red and there's
nothing I can do to save you.
Most people wake up before their monster catches
them. They have to, because they wouldn't be able to
take what happens next. It would break them.
I love you, M, because your monster has caught you.
But it has never broken you. You are still the kindest,
most gentle, loving person I have ever met and
I can't wait to see you when I come home. Our home. I
just want to be home.
Ugh. I'm freaking out right now and I wish they would
fucking shut up out there! I wish you'd at least just
write me a text and say, "Shut up, leave me alone."
Home. I'll be home soon. And I'll be there for you,
however you need me because home is a strengthening
thing. Ha! Remember that guy? "Home is a
strengthening thing." I can't wait to have him on our
show so he can tell us all about the Japanese honeyb–
(Pause)
This isn't right.
This isn't right, is it
Something's
(Stops recording. Starts calling M again.)
Come on. Come on. Pick up the fucking phone.

(Blackout)

Scene 12

*(Back in the apartment. Silence. Darkness. Just the sound of
rain)*

(The sound of the bedroom door opening.)

(After some time)

JEFF: Your phone won't stop ringing.

(Lights rise [though not much—it's still dark] to find JEFF standing by M's cot, holding a knife over M's face.)

(JEFF's floorlamp is also back, as well as some other little features of his previous décor.)

(M is awake. M sees the knife but barely reacts. M is in a lot of pain and discomfort.)

JEFF: It's been ringing all night. I almost answered it half a dozen times.

Six

Five

(After four, with every number, he lifts a finger off the knife.)

Four, three, two, one

(When he gets to 1, instead of the knife falling, he opens his hand and reveals the knife has been glued to his palm.)

Zero

I can't stop thinking about glue. I'm sure you can imagine.

(He goes and turns the lamp on.)

I had a sister. And she used to cut herself up. No matter what mom told her, begged her, she'd fall back into the habit. I have this crystal clear memory walking by her room one day and she was crying. "I can't stop." I can't stop.

Why is it so hard to change? Why is it so hard to get… unstuck.

(He rips off the knife from his palm. It hurts. A lot. It tears a good chunk of his skin off in the process. He seethes in pain and cradles his hand. Close to tears; genuine)

Oh, that hurts.

I'm really sorry for how I acted today. About all this. Doing this to you.

I'm really sorry.

Oh

Oh, it hurts

(M watches JEFF with almost sympathy. He's in a really bad place. Pause. When M speaks, it's cheery and upbeat.)

M: Hey

If you go to the bathroom, there's a bottle of oxycodone in the medicine cabinet.

JEFF: Is that—?

M: It's for pain. It's awesome.

JEFF: I don't usually like to take that kinda stuff, but…

M: Might help.

(JEFF considers, then goes into the bathroom.)

JEFF: *(In the other room)* Do you mind if I use one of your towels?

M: Hey, it's your house, too!

(That makes JEFF SO happy. He bounds out, giddy, holding a bottle of pills, with a towel wrapped around his hand.)

JEFF: It *is*, isn't it? Thanks!

M: Get some water, too.

JEFF: Right! Want some?

M: Sure. Thanks!

(JEFF goes to the kitchen.)

(Thunder. M winces in pain.)

(JEFF comes back with a glass of water with a straw in it.)

M: You found our straws.

JEFF: It's a fun idea, having straws.

M: Right?

JEFF: *(Re the pills)* Uh, how many should I *(take)*?

M: If it hurts really bad?

JEFF: Yeah

M: You can do as many as five. Sometimes even six. To start.

JEFF: …they look kind of big. I'll just do one for now. I'm a lightweight.

(He takes a pill. Swallows it with the help of some water.)

M: You know what, I'll take one, too. Thanks. (M *dry swallows a pill.)*
Hate the rain.

JEFF: Me, too.

M: So, was that true? What you just told me about your sister?

JEFF: My…?

M: The cutting. You said your sister—

JEFF: Oh. Yeah. I
(Barely audible) I don't want to talk about that
He starts to stare off into space again, holding an earlobe.

M: *(Not wanting him to disappear)* No, no, it's okay, it's okay!
Hey. We don't have to talk about that

JEFF: Sorry, whenever I really think about my family, it kind of overloads me, like I just… *(Makes a frazzled, short-circuiting gesture)* I turn off. It's weird.

M: I noticed. Family, right? Ugh.

JEFF: Ugh. Yeah. *(He sits.)*
I really messed up, M.
I don't know what to do about all this.

M: Have another pill. It'll help

JEFF: I dunno, I don't wanna get addicted or anything.

M: Look at that bottle. I've had them for years. Would I still have them if they were really addictive?

JEFF: I guess not

M: And they help with all kinds of things. Rainy days. When I'm sad. I had an accident a little while ago, they help with that, too. It's cool.

JEFF: Like a car accident?

M: No.

JEFF: I get hit by cars a lot. No fun.
Maybe I'll have another one.
(He swallows another one.)
I think I'm feeling a little better.

M: See?

JEFF: Can I be honest with you?
You are really good at, at this. At… *(Nods to the cot)* being here. The past two days, I don't want you to think I haven't noticed, or that I don't appreciate it. I can only imagine how crazy this must be.
But you're
Thanks

M: What's your favorite song?

JEFF: Huh?

M: To, uh, "sing" to. What's your favorite song to sing to?

JEFF: Oh!
Purple Rain. Those are some really beautiful chords. Only four chords in the whole song. You can sing a lot over them. It's the same chords as *Faithfully,* actually, did you know that?

M: Wanna put it on right now?

JEFF: *(A sudden realization)* Hey! How's your radio thing? That project you guys were working on

M: It's

Well, it's kind of on hold at the *moment*. *("Because I'm trapped, you asshole.")*

JEFF: Because G has to go out of town a lot?

M: Yeah…

JEFF: *(An important question)* Can I ask…Is it…*fun*?

M: It's

It's a new start for us. We wanted // to start our lives over again. You know, you

JEFF: *(Singing—quietly, almost to himself)* "When the working day is done, oh, Girls just wanna have fuh-un…"

M: Okay. Jesus, never mind, asshole!

JEFF: Sorry, I just got the urge to sing something. I'm

M: Right. Go fuck yourself.

JEFF: No, I'm—

M: GO. FUCK. YOUR. SELF.

JEFF: Jeez, I—

M: For a *second* there I thought you might *actually* be capable of feeling things but I guess I was wrong

JEFF: What does *that* mean?

M: People who ask questions but then don't care about the answers—?

JEFF: I care, I was listening!

M: Yeah, but there are two ways to listen. You can listen like you're hungry or you can listen like you're thirsty.

Hungry people listen but they're always looking for the next thing they can just bite into and chew. It's loud and it's ugly.

If you're *thirsty* you don't make a noise. You just drink it in.

JEFF: I didn't mean to chew! I just get sad sometimes and I need to sing! I'm sorry!

(M *starts to laugh.*)

M: Jeeeeeeeeeeeeeeeeesus

JEFF: I don't want you to be mad at me!

M: Welp. This is a real crisis point in our relationship.

JEFF: (*Sincerely pouting, stomping in place*) Mannnnnnnn!

M: Okay, fucking calm down—

JEFF: It's just, there was a reason I asked you just now if it's "fun!" I was trying to

M: What?

JEFF: I know you're gonna take offense to this, but…I feel like I *recognize* something in you

M: You recognize something // in me

JEFF: Like, a, a *distance*
I'm not trying to say that we're the same picture.
But we might have been…drawn from the same perspective
Even when we first met! I could just tell there was—I could just tell *fun* isn't easy for you. Fun is hard. Am I right?
(*Beat. He is.*)
I thought, [s]he doesn't really want to be here, in this apartment. I mean, maybe [s]he *wants* to want it, but

M: I don't want anything, okay? I just want to stop feeling like my life is a snow globe full of shit that's shaken up again and again and again

JEFF: (*"I know EXACTLY how you feel"*) Yes!
I could see that coming off of you like, like stink waves in a cartoon!

M: Great

JEFF: No, no, it's not a bad thing! You hide it really well; I don't think anyone would notice! It's just…there's like a secret language, and only people who've *really* been through bad stuff can speak it. Right? Haven't you ever noticed that? Ugh, I'm probably not making any sense—

M: No, you…
…I know what you mean.

JEFF: You do?

M: *(Not wanting to admit it)* …yeah

JEFF: Yay! I mean, I *thought* you might. *(He rattles the pill bottle by way of explanation.)*
Do you mind if I *(have another)*?

M: No, go for it. Have // a few

JEFF: *(Popping a pill as he speaks)* But, by the way, it's not other people's fault for not speaking that language, they just, they *don't know*, right?

M: Yeah.
Right.
They don't know.
Even if they love you…they still don't know.

*(*JEFF *sits down next to the cot, leaning his head against it, buddy-buddy.)*

JEFF: Oh, it's so good to talk about this with someone else!
You know what I think it is? I think they think it's like a wound or a cut or something. They think you *heal*.

M: Ha! No such thing.

JEFF: There's no such thing! They just think it'll leave a little scar and be all nice and tidy and healed. But you don't heal, you, like, I dunno, you—

M: Mutate.

(Beat)

JEFF: YESSSSSSS
It's like growing another arm that you have to learn
how to move and, and use and

M: And if you mutate enough times, you're not even
the same species anymore. You don't care about the
same things—you can't. They're not *for* your kind.

JEFF: "Sorry, sir, you've got too many arms"

M: And you wanna be like, y'know…well, I can't really
do it, but imagine, like, twenty-two middle fingers

JEFF: *(In awe)* Whoa—twenty-two middle fingers?

M: At *least*
I'm a fucking megaoctopus.

JEFF: Wow.
Hey, do you want another *(pill)*?

M: Sure.

(JEFF gives M one.)

M: *(Pill in mouth)* You should have another, too. The
more you have, the better you'll

JEFF: Okay

*(JEFF goes to get the glass of water and M just dry swallows
the pill. He takes one and drinks.)*

JEFF: So, here's a question. Do you ever think about
killing yourself? Ending it all?

M: Sure.

JEFF: Yeah?

M: Shit yeah
Sometimes I even have to get up and, and walk
around, like physically shake it off. It creeps up behind

me and puts its hands on my shoulders and if I don't move around I get scared that it's just going to…push

JEFF: Wow

M: (*Like it's hilarious gossip*) And, man, getting pushed is noooo fun. Hahah—like, *one* of my octopus arms? This performance group I used to be a part of? We did a ton of stupid shit. And one day, we took some of the wrong stuff, I think it mighta been laced with PCP or something—maybe not, who knows—but one of my closest friends started getting crazy sexual with me. I told her no and she fucking lost it, she started hitting me with everything she could find, her fists, books, her fucking iron, and then she just <u>shoved</u> me out of her open window. Thankfully it was the second floor, but. Splat. Crackle. Pop.

(*Beat*)

JEFF: (*Deeply shocked*) This was a *friend* of yours?

M: Close friend. Real close.

JEFF: What's their name?

M: Berit.

JEFF: Berit

M: Oh! And now, haha, she and her fucking partner Michael? They spend all their time just posting shit about me online. Like, how I made it all up, I just got fucked up and fell, and it's all my fault they stopped actively producing shit. Cuz I got a lot of money in a settlement, her parents are fucking rich, but they're still like, "Just thinking today about liars who ruin lives." Or, "A true friend knows how to forgive." Or, "Wouldn't it be great awful things actually *did* happen to awful people?" Fucking petty fucking cunts. Pop! Out comes another arm!

JEFF: (*Crying; deeply upset*) That's

M, I'm so sorry.
That's so unfair

M: Unfair! Ha! Just life, buddy!

JEFF: No, it's not, it // shouldn't be

M: That's *all* life is, just a steadily progressing chain of
horrible things

I mean, look at me right now! It. Always. Gets. Worse!

JEFF: But, I mean
You and I just met. *We* meant nothing to each other
beyond the *possibility*, the *potential* for some deeper
connection. This Berit woman, she was your friend.
You felt safe in her presence!

M: Big mistake—

JEFF: NO! IT SHOULDN'T BE A MISTAKE! TO FEEL
SAFE? TO LOVE, TO TRUST??
It should be sacred and SHE abused that!
Not everybody gets friends, and for her to just
I'm so mad I'm like shaking
(Starting to cry) I'm so sorry
I'm so
God

M: Take a few more pills! You'll feel better! You'll //
think clearly.

JEFF: I DON'T WANT TO FEEL BETTER
I think:
I think, this isn't right of me.
This isn't fair. To either of us. We've both been through
too much.

M: You're right
Take a few more pills

JEFF: *(Swaying on his feet)* No, I actually feel kinda dizzy
so…I think I'm gonna go to bed.

But tomorrow I'm going to take care of everything.
Okay?

I promise. Tomorrow I'm gonna stop *this (Gesturing to the cot)*

M: *(Hope)* You are?

JEFF: Yeah. Yeah, we can't keep doing this.

M: You're right! Thank you!
And it's going to be okay.
We're both going to be okay, I promise—

JEFF: Before tonight, I used to think that pain could be like a house. You move in…and then you start to know the place. You even fall in love with its little quirks. But you can't force someone to make a place their home. Can you?

M: No

JEFF: No.
So I'm going to kill you in the morning.
Okay.

(JEFF exits into the bedroom. Lights fade.)

Scene 13

(Morning light streams into the living room.)

(M continues to work on getting free. M can lift even more off of the cot. M snaps back down to the cot when JEFF enters. He's getting hurriedly dressed for work:)

JEFF: Ahh! I slept too late! I never sleep too late! Ahh!
So
I had a weird thought last night. You know how, like, when celebrities die they always say it's in threes? I wonder if
(As he speaks, he goes to another room and gets a yellow reflective vest bearing the word SEAMLESS)

What if, when you become a celebrity—y'know, when
you finally *commit*—what if they give you a number.
They just hand it to you with the rest of your celebrity
stuff, your, your packet. And, only two other celebrities
have that same number—old, young, doesn't matter,
it's totally random. No one talks about it. But when
one of the other people with your number dies, maybe
someone calls you and says, "They were a," y'know,
"8-4-2 also." And then you know you've gotta die, too.
But it's all part of the deal.
Wouldn't that be crazy?
Heh
Anyway
I have to go to work today. I took too many days off so
I'm going to get in trouble. Plus I could use the money.
(*He puts on a bicycle helmet.*)
 Boom.
What do you think? I don't like the vest much but.
Well.
Keeps me in shape at least!
And it's kinda fun, as far as work goes. Get a little peek
in on other people's lives, even if it's just for a few
seconds. You know?
(*Beat*)
…are you…mad at me?
Oh. This is about killing you. Isn't it.
It's going to be painless. I've done it before, a buncha
times. I know what I'm doing. You probably won't
believe me but I really do care, I really do want
And, after all you said last night, I just hate myself for
thinking this was fair of me.
Do you want me to do it now or when I get back from
work?
I slept later than I meant to, I figured I'd be able to take
care of everything before work, but now I'm running

behind. But I also don't want to leave you here, uncomfortable if

M: I'm fine.

JEFF: Are you sure? Because I can do everything I need to, I just don't know if I have time to clean up and not be late. I left my bike at the restaurant, so I gotta walk over and

M: Don't worry about it, I can wait.

JEFF: Okay! Okay! If you don't mind, then. (*He runs to the bathroom. Swishes some water in his mouth and spits. Comes back.*) I appreciate it.

I'll be back soon!

Thanks!

(*He scurries out.*)

(*As soon as* JEFF'*s gone,* M *gets to work, trying to lift off the cot. We hear the slowly growing sound of rushing air that turns into a creature's growl, the more* M *struggles. It hurts. It hurts so fucking much. Too much.* M *can't do it. But* M *tries again.*)

M: Please, please

(M'*s exhausted. Out of breath. Close to tears. This might be* M'*s only chance.*)

(*All the sound cuts out.*)

(*The sound of a key in the door.* M *immediately ceases.*)

(*The door opens.*)

G: Hello?

(*Closes the door*)

Hello? Baby, you (*home*)

M: (*Barely a whisper*) Baby—?

(G *sees* M. *They lock eyes for a moment and are both dumbfounded.*)

(*Beat*)

G: Oh my god

(G *drops her/his/their bag [maybe under the cot?] and rushes over to* M.)

G: Oh my god   M: You're home
What happened?   Is this real?
What happened to you?   Is this real?
Oh, god, oh, baby, what
happened to you
WHAT HAPPENED TO
YOU

M: I got glued to a bed.
(*Starts laughing, hearing that outloud.*)

G: Oh my god
Who did this to you?
Was it Berit? // How do we get you out of this?

M: No
Oh god it hurts so bad
Haaahaha

G: Baby

M: I think you need to cut me out of it. There's, there's
a knife thing, I think it's in the kitchen
Haha—I got fucking glued to a bed, baby
Oh, I'm so glad you're here
You're really here, right?

(G *is panickedly looking for the putty knife.* G *comes back with it.*)

G: Okay, okay, what do I do, I just

(G *starts trying to cut around the glue. One of* M's *arms is eventually freed.*)

M: Yeah, be careful
I love you

G: I love you, I'm so sorry I left you

I'm so sorry, I'm so sorry, / / I'm so sorry, I'm so sorry

M: Hey, hey, hey. Shush. You have nothing to be sorry for. Baby. Haha—this where I live, I live here

G: What?

(The sound of a key in the door. Since G didn't lock the door, JEFF accidentally does. He tries to open it and he bumps into it and drops his keys.)

M: Hide. Run.

G: What Where	JEFF: *(Outside)* What the Aw, man
M: The bedroom. Hide. I'll tell you when to come out And take that knife. We're gonna kill him GO	Great. Good job, dummy.

(G runs into the bedroom. We hear the closet door close.)

(The front door opens and JEFF walks in.)

JEFF: Did I forget to lock the door? Oh, man, I'm losing it.

So

I got a few blocks away and then I had to stop and come back. This is wrong of me. Making you wait. You've gotta be in so much pain and, and, and, I should just get it done now.

M: What about your job?

JEFF: *(Surprised at M's response)* Oh

Well, if I get fired…so be it. I kind of deserve it, don't I? This whole thing is making me take stock.

I have a lot of anger in me. Hate, really. I should call it what it is.

I am just pounding with hate. For, for this city, for myself, for the people who have come in and out of my life. But now—now I have it for the people who have come in and out of your life, too! To have gone through what you've gone through, to, to have been hurt and abused and, I mean, you're already differently oriented, you're already systematically oppressed, it's fucking, fucking, fucking awful, so, no way, no fucking way am I letting you sit here in pain, no! NO WAY. Because, why, because I'm worried about my fucking floor? Because it'll smell bad when I get home? This is bullshit of me! I'm sorry for the strong language but I expect fucking better of // myself!

(JEFF's ranting, but he doesn't see G's bag. Near the end, though, he gets close and M jumps in.)

M: Hey

JEFF: What

M: I think I'd like to sing a little?

JEFF: Excuse me?

M: Is that okay? You're right—and you've inspired me. I mean
I've never fit in either. I get it. I'd like to sing. With you

JEFF: That
Sounds
Awesome!
Um
(He runs over to the stereo.)
What do you want to

M: You pick.

JEFF: And then we'll

M: Whatever you need to do.

(JEFF puts on a C D. Let's say it's Purple Rain for now.)

JEFF: Okay

M: Do you, will you sing first?

JEFF: *(Overjoyed)* WHAT Okay! Is this what having a roommate is like?

M: It can be.
Take it away.

(JEFF sings a verse from a different song, as per his style. M joins him. When the verse is complete:)

JEFF: It's kinda fun, right?

M: I just have one request.

JEFF: What's that?

M: Sing to me like I'm your father.

(Beat)

JEFF: My

M: Sing to me like I'm your father. Come on. Put everything you feel about your father, or your mother, or your sister—give it all you've got to me. We're family now. How do you think you'd sing to them?

JEFF: My
(He stares off into space, struck dumb. Holds his earlobe.)

M: No? Okay, I'll go then
(Singing)
DO IT NOWWWW
NOW
COME ON OUT AND DOO ITTTTT
(Beat. What the fuck?)
RUN OUT AND DO ITT
NOWWWWWW
PLEASEEE
STAB HIM IN THE BACK OF THE NECK

(JEFF starts to come out of it.)

JEFF: I don't know that song.

M: WHY
WHY AREN'T YOU
COME ONNNnn

(JEFF *turns the music down, not off entirely.* M *is utterly defeated, realizing her mistake.*)

JEFF: I don't know if you understand
You're supposed to sing an *actual* song.

M: *(To herself)* The fucking closet
Oh god the closet

JEFF: What

M: We soundproofed the closet.
(Starts to laugh again.)

JEFF: You did? You...changed that, too?

M: Ha! Oh, yeah, we changed the fuck out of it.
Haaaaha
(When the laughing dies down)
Can you get me some water?

JEFF: Yeah. Sure.
(He leaves for the kitchen.)

M: Fuck. Fuck.

(JEFF *comes back. He has the bottle of pills in his hand and also a paintbrush with adhesive coated on it.*)

JEFF: I told you what would happen. I told you what would happen if you changed things.

(JEFF *puts a few pills in* M's *mouth, throws the bottle away, then squeezes* M's *mouth with one hand and coats adhesive all over* M's *mouth with the other.*)

(M's *freed arm comes up and tries to fight but it's no use.*)

JEFF: How did *that* happen?
Okay, shhh, shhh

(M *starts to quiet down.* M *has no choice but to swallow the pills.*)

JEFF: Okay. Well, I guess it's time to do this, then.
It's gonna be quick. I promise.
(*He exits to the kitchen. He comes back out with a new tarp, still in the package. He opens it up, lays it down. He kneels down to* M *and speaks calmly, lovingly, quietly. He really is good at this.*)
I know you're scared. But drink. We're going to do your wrists and the pills will help make it painless. I'll get that nice, sharp knife and I'll warm it under the tap, okay? Just remember, it's a thing you always wanted to try, right? If you're scared I want you to burrow into that. You're just trying something new. That's always scary. Don't think of the consequences, focus on the new. Feel those hands on your shoulders…and don't shake them off this time.
(*He goes back into the kitchen.*)

(*After a few beats,* G *quietly sneaks out of the bedroom.*)

G: (*Quietly*) Is he gone? I couldn't hear—

JEFF: (*Offstage*) I can't find that good putty knife, it was shar—

(JEFF *comes back in. He and* G *stare at each other for a good moment, each unsure how to react.*)

(JEFF *calmly reaches over and turns up the stereo. Then he chases* G *into the bedroom.* M *watches helplessly.*)

(*Finally they end up back in the living room.* G *is moving backwards, trying to avoid* JEFF. G *swings the putty knife at him and he jumps out of the way each time.*)

G: HELP!
HELP!

(JEFF *takes off his helmet. Instead of going after G, he cracks M in the face with his helmet. G screams and for the first time heads for him instead of away.*)

G: No!

(JEFF *whips the helmet at G's face. G isn't expecting it and takes the blow full on. G drops the knife.* JEFF *drops the helmet and starts to strangle G.*)

(*There's a knock on the door.*)

NEIGHBOR: Hey, sorry, can you turn the music down, we can hear it in the hallway

(G *and* JEFF *bump into the stereo—it falls to the floor and breaks. The harsh buzz of bees is barely heard under all of this—or maybe it's just the broken speakers.*)

NEIGHBOR: (*Voice retreating*) Thank you!

(M *is trying to see clearly again. Seeing G in danger, M gives it all one final burst of effort. With the freed arm M is able to get some leverage and RIPS forward. The tearing noise is nauseating. The pain is immense, but the pills have helped to dull it. And, of course, M's mouth is glued shut so there is no real scream. Unfortunately, M's motor skills are shot and M has been lying down for days. M collapses to the ground.*)

(M *finds the putty knife on the floor. M crawls towards it, grabs it, then crawls towards G and* JEFF. *M plunges the putty knife into* JEFF's *side.*)

(*He screams. M continues to stab him. G and M both get on top of him, battering him, stabbing him. They swarm all over him. He's overcome, dazed, barely able to fight back.*)

(*He weakly manages to crawl away, arbitrarily heading toward the bathroom.*)

G: (*Ragged*) You fucking bastard
Look what you did to her [him].
You're gonna hurt

I am going to hurt you

(G *drags* JEFF *into the bathroom. We hear the water turn on in the tub. The buzz of bees intensifies under it.*)

G: I'M GONNA HURT YOU

(*After a few seconds,* JEFF *starts to shriek as he's horribly burned by the scalding water. He shrieks desperately, in unspeakable pain…then quiets.*)

(*After a moment,* G *stumbles out of the bathroom and towards* M.)

(*They hold each other. Pause*)

G: Hi
Oh, your poor face.
I love you.
We're okay. We're okay.
Okay.
Can you stand? Let's

(G *moves* M *to the couch [or somewhere else with their backs to the bathroom].*)

G: Okay. I'm going to call the police now. Okay?

(M *nods.*)

G: And we're gonna be okay now. Okay?

(M *tries to nod, but can't.*)

G: We're gonna be okay
We're gonna heal and we're gonna get past this

(G *strokes* M's *hair for a moment. Then* G *goes to their bag to get a cell phone.*)

(JEFF *enters from the bathroom. His skin is scalded bright, bright red. His face is a red nightmare of shining, raw flesh. He walks towards them quickly.*)

(*Blackout*)

Scene 14

(The apartment is a little cleaner. JEFF *is still in pretty bad shape, but this is a couple days later. M and G are nowhere to be found.)*

*(*JEFF *is on a phone call. At one point, while he speaks, he walks to the handprint on the wall.)*

JEFF: Well, I don't know what to tell you, Rogelio! I came by to see if any of my mail had shown up and the place was totally empty. They left the door wide open, all their stuff was gone! So, so, so, you'd be an idiot to not take me up on my offer. I'll go month-to-month, I'll sign a lease. You can even consider me a subletter—we met a few times, we were cool.

Whatever. But it's up to you. If you want to just let the place stay empty

Yeah

I mean, I don't want to gossip. I think there were drug problems. Big ones. Did you know the [brunette] one, there was PCP, there was

Oh yeah, they told me *all* about it. And abusive exes. It was very disturbing. Maybe if you weren't so concerned about raising the rent and had done a little background checking, you might have

You're right, I'm sorry

Yeah

Yeah

(He touches the handprint. Then, still speaking, he picks up a hammer and a nail.)

Hey, listen, you're gonna want to look into replacing the tub, too. I'm happy to live with it as is, but I think they did some, some pretty, uh, pretty disturbing things in there. Like dressing animals, even. It's gross, I don't know where you found these guys

Come by if you want. I don't want to put you in an
awkward position. I just care about the apartment,
I lived here a long time, Rogelio. You know, a loyal
tenant has gotta be worth something.
Okay, I gotta go. Think about it, okay?

*(He hangs up. He hammers a nail into the wall above the
handprint. The he hangs an empty picture frame on the wall,
framing the handprint. He admires it.)*

JEFF: It's actually kinda

*(The buzzer rings. He goes to the buzzer, still holding the
hammer.)*

JEFF: Yellow?

VOICE: *(Female)* Hi. Uh. Is this Jeff? This is Berit. I'm
here for

JEFF: Yes! M and G's friend. Hi!

VOICE: Yeah. Hi. Almost didn't come, but, uh

JEFF: No, they're so glad you're here. I'm so glad you
decided to come. Come on in—

(He buzzes her in. Immediately; quietly)

—you petty, lying cunt

*(JEFF waits by the door, holding the hammer. Starts to sing
to himself. The sound of buzzing insects begins to grow.)*

JEFF: You'd be so nice to come home to
You'd be so nice by the fire
While the breeze on high, sang a lullaby
You'd be

(There's a knock at the door.)

(Blackout

END OF PLAY